Practical
Pasta & Italian

p^3

This is a P³ Book
This edition published in 2003

P³
Queen Street House
4 Queen Street
Bath BA1 1HE, UK

ISBN: 1-40542-310-2

Manufactured in China

NOTE

Cup measurements in this book are for American cups.
This book also uses imperial and metric measurements. Follow the same units
of measurement throughout; do not mix imperial and metric.
All spoon measurements are level: teaspoons are assumed to be 5 ml, and
tablespoons are assumed to be 15 ml. Unless otherwise stated,
milk is assumed to be whole milk, eggs and individual vegetables such as potatoes
are medium, and pepper is freshly ground black pepper.

The nutritional information provided for each recipe is per serving or per person.
Optional ingredients, variations, or serving suggestions have
not been included in the calculations. The times given for each recipe are an approximate
guide only because the preparation times may differ according to the techniques used by
different people and the cooking times may vary as a result of the type of oven used.

Recipes using raw or very lightly cooked eggs should be
avoided by infants, the elderly, pregnant women, convalescents,
and anyone suffering from an illness.

Contents

Introduction

Pasta has existed in one form or another since the days of the Roman Empire and remains one of the most versatile ingredients in the kitchen. It can be combined with almost anything from meat to fish, vegetables to fruit, and is even delicious served with simple herb sauces. No pantry should be without a supply of dried pasta, which, combined with a few other stock ingredients, can be turned into a mouthwatering and nutritious meal within minutes.

Why eat pasta?

Most pasta is made from durum wheat flour and contains protein and carbohydrates. It is a good source of slow-release energy and has the additional advantage of being good value for money.

Varieties

There is an enormous range of different types of pasta, some of which are listed on the opposite page. Many are available both dried and fresh. Unless you have access to a good Italian delicatessen, it is probably not worth buying fresh, unfilled pasta, but even large stores sell high-quality tortellini, capelletti, ravioli, and agnolotti. Best of all is to make fresh pasta at home. It takes a little time, but is quite easy and well worth the effort. You can mix the dough by hand or prepare it in a food processor if you prefer.

Colors and flavors

Pasta may be colored and flavored with extra ingredients that are usually added with the beaten egg:
Black: add 1 tsp squid or cuttlefish ink.
Green: add 4 oz/115 g well-drained cooked spinach when kneading.
Purple: work 1 large, cooked beet in a food processor and add with an extra ½ cup of flour.
Red: add 2 tbsp tomato paste.

Cooking pasta

Always use a large pan for cooking pasta and bring lightly salted water to a boil. Add the pasta and 1 tbsp olive oil, but do not cover or the water will boil over. Quickly bring the water back to a rolling boil and avoid overcooking. When the pasta is tender, but still firm to the bite, drain and toss with butter, olive oil, or your prepared sauce, and serve as soon as possible.

The cooking times given here are guidelines only:

Fresh, unfilled pasta:	2–3 minutes
Fresh, filled pasta:	8–10 minutes
Dried, unfilled pasta:	10–12 minutes
Dried, filled pasta:	15–20 minutes

Basic Pasta Dough

If you wish to make your own pasta for the dishes in this book, follow this simple recipe.

SERVES 4

INGREDIENTS

3½ cups durum wheat flour

4 eggs, lightly beaten

1 tbsp olive oil

salt

1 Lightly flour a counter. Sift the flour with a pinch of salt into a mound. Make a well in the center and add the beaten eggs and olive oil.

2 Using a fork or your fingertips, gradually work the mixture until the ingredients are combined. Knead vigorously for 10–15 minutes.

3 Set the dough aside to rest for 25 minutes, before rolling it out as thinly and evenly as possible and using as desired.

Types of pasta

There are as many as 200 different pasta shapes and about three times as many names for them. New shapes are being designed—and named—all the time and the same shape may be called a different name in different regions of Italy.

anelli, anellini: *small rings for soup*

bucatini: *long, medium-thick tubes*

cannelloni: *large, thick, round pasta tubes*

capelli d'angelo: *thin strands of "angel hair"*

conchiglie: *ridged shells*

conchigliette: *small shells*

cresti di gallo: *curve-shaped*

ditali, ditalini: *short tubes*

eliche: *loose spirals*

farfalle: *bows*

fettuccine: *medium ribbons*

fusilli: *spirals*

gemelli: *two pieces wrapped together as "twins"*

lasagna: *flat, rectangular sheets*

linguine: *long, flat ribbons*

lumache: *snail-shaped shells*

lumaconi: *big shells*

macaroni: *long-cut or short-cut tubes*

orecchiette: *ear-shaped*

penne: *quill-shaped*

rigatoni: *thick, ridged tubes*

spaghetti: *fine or medium rods*

tagliarini: *thin ribbons*

tagliatelle: *broad ribbons*

vermicelli: *fine pasta, usually folded into skeins*

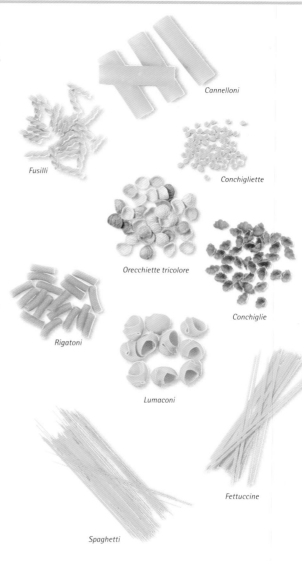

Cannelloni

Fusilli

Conchigliette

Orecchiette tricolore

Conchiglie

Rigatoni

Lumaconi

Fettuccine

Spaghetti

KEY	
	Simplicity level 1–3 (1 easiest, 3 slightly harder)
	Preparation time
	Cooking time

Brown Lentil & Pasta Soup

In Italy, this soup is called *Minestrade Lentiche*. A minestra is a soup cooked with pasta; here, farfalline, a small bow-shaped variety, is used.

NUTRITIONAL INFORMATION

Calories 225	Sugars 1g
Protein 13g	Fat 8g
Carbohydrate . . . 27g	Saturates 3g

 5 mins   🕐 25 mins

SERVES 4

I N G R E D I E N T S

4 strips lean bacon, cut into small squares

1 onion, chopped

2 garlic cloves, crushed

2 celery stalks, chopped

1¾ oz/50 g farfalline or spaghetti, broken into small pieces

14 oz/400 g canned brown lentils, drained

5 cups hot vegetable or ham bouillon

2 tbsp chopped fresh mint

1 Place the bacon in a large skillet together with the onions, garlic, and celery. Dry cook for 4–5 minutes, stirring, until the onion is tender and the bacon is just beginning to brown.

2 Add the pasta to the skillet and cook, stirring, for about 1 minute, to coat the pasta thoroughly in the oil.

3 Add the brown lentils and the vegetable or ham bouillon and bring the mixture to a boil. Lower the heat and let simmer for 12–15 minutes, or until the pasta is tender.

4 Remove the skillet from the heat and stir in the chopped fresh mint.

5 Transfer the soup to warm soup bowls and serve immediately.

COOK'S TIP

If you prefer to use dried lentils, add the bouillon before the pasta and cook for 1–1¼ hours, until the lentils are tender. Add the pasta and cook for another 12–15 minutes.

  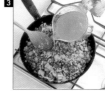

Pistou

This hearty soup of beans and vegetables is from Nice and gets its name from the fresh basil sauce stirred in at the last minute.

10 mins   25 mins

SERVES 6

I N G R E D I E N T S

2 young carrots

1 lb/450 g potatoes

7 oz/200 g fresh peas in their shells

7 oz/200 g thin green beans

5½ oz/150 g young zucchini

2 tbsp olive oil

1 garlic clove, crushed

1 large onion, finely chopped

10½ cups vegetable bouillon or water

1 bouquet garni, or 2 fresh parsley sprigs
    and 1 bay leaf tied in a 3-inch/7.5-cm ·
    piece of celery stalk

3 oz/85 g dried small soup pasta

1 large tomato, skinned, seeded, and
    chopped or diced

freshly pared Parmesan cheese, to serve

P I S T O U   S A U C E

2¾ oz/75 g fresh basil leaves

1 garlic clove

5 tbsp fruity extra-virgin olive oil

salt and pepper

1 To make the pistou sauce, put the basil leaves, garlic, and olive oil in a food processor, and process until well blended. Season with salt and pepper to taste. Transfer to a bowl, cover with plastic wrap, and chill until required.

2 Peel the carrots, cut them in half lengthwise, then slice them. Peel the potatoes and cut into fourths lengthwise, then slice. Set aside in a bowl of water until ready to use, to prevent discoloration.

3 Shell the fresh peas. Trim the green beans and cut them into 1-inch/2.5-cm pieces. Cut the zucchini in half lengthwise, then slice crosswise.

4 Heat the oil in a large pan or flameproof casserole. Add the garlic and cook for 2 minutes, stirring. Add the onion and continue cooking for 2 minutes, until soft. Add the carrots and potatoes and stir for about 30 seconds.

5 Pour in the bouillon and bring to a boil. Lower the heat, partially cover, and simmer for 8 minutes, until the vegetables are starting to become tender.

6 Stir in the peas, beans, zucchini, bouquet garni, pasta, and tomato. Season and cook for 4 minutes, or until the vegetables and pasta are tender. Stir in the pistou sauce and serve with Parmesan.

Lemon & Chicken Soup

This delicately flavored summer soup is surprisingly easy to make, and tastes absolutely delicious.

NUTRITIONAL INFORMATION

Calories	506	Sugars	4g
Protein	19g	Fat	31g
Carbohydrate	41g	Saturates	19g

5–10 mins   1¼ hrs

SERVES 4

I N G R E D I E N T S

4 tbsp butter

8 shallots, thinly sliced

2 carrots, thinly sliced

2 celery stalks, thinly sliced

8 oz/225 g boned chicken breasts, finely chopped

3 lemons

5 cups chicken bouillon

8 oz/225 g dried spaghetti, broken into small pieces

⅔ cup heavy cream

salt and white pepper

TO GARNISH

sprigs of fresh parsley

fresh lemon slices, halved

1 Melt the butter in a large pan. Add the shallots, carrots, celery, and chicken and cook over low heat, stirring occasionally, for 8 minutes.

2 Thinly pare the lemons and then blanch the zest in boiling water for 3 minutes. Squeeze the juice from the lemons.

3 Add the lemon rind and juice and the chicken bouillon to the pan. Bring slowly to a boil over low heat. Simmer for 40 minutes, stirring occasionally.

4 Add the spaghetti to the pan and cook for 15 minutes. Season to taste with salt and white pepper and add the cream. Heat through, but do not let the soup boil or it will curdle.

5 Pour the soup into a large serving bowl or individual soup bowls, garnish with sprigs of parsley and half slices of lemon, and serve immediately.

COOK'S TIP

You can prepare this soup up to the end of step 3 in advance, so that all you need do before serving is heat it through before adding the pasta and the finishing touches.

Spinach & Herb Orzo

Serve this vibrant green pasta dish with any broiled meat or seafood.
Orzo, shaped like grains of barley, is popular in southern Italy and Greece.

NUTRITIONAL INFORMATION			
Calories 304	Sugars 8g		
Protein 12g	Fat 6g		
Carbohydrate . . . 54g	Saturates 1g		

15–20 mins   10 mins

SERVES 4

I N G R E D I E N T S

1 tsp salt

9 oz/250 g dried orzo

7 oz/200 g baby spinach leaves

5½ oz/150 g arugula

1 oz/25 g fresh flatleaf parsley

1 oz/25 g fresh cilantro

4 scallions

2 tbsp extra-virgin olive oil

1 tbsp garlic-flavored olive oil

pepper

T O   S E R V E

radicchio or other lettuce leaves

2 oz/55 g feta cheese, well drained and
crumbled (optional)

lemon slices

1 Bring 2 pans of water to a boil, and
put 12 ice cubes in a bowl of cold
water. Add the salt and orzo to one of the
pans, return to a boil, and cook for 8–10
minutes, or according to package
instructions, until the pasta is tender.

2 Meanwhile, remove any tough spinach
stems. Rinse the leaves thoroughly to
remove any grit. Chop the arugula, parsley,
cilantro, and green parts of the scallions.

3 Put the spinach, arugula, parsley,
cilantro, and scallions in the other pan
of boiling water and blanch for 15 seconds.
Drain and transfer to the iced water to
preserve the color.

4 When the spinach, herbs, and scallions
are cool, squeeze out all the excess
water. Transfer to a small food processor
and process. Add the olive oil and
garlic-flavored oil and process again until
the spinach mixture is well blended.

5 Drain the orzo well and stir in
the spinach mixture. Toss well and
adjust the seasoning.

6 Line a serving platter with radicchio
leaves and pile the orzo on top.
Sprinkle with feta cheese, if desired, and
garnish with lemon slices. Serve hot or let
cool to room temperature.

Filled Eggplants

Combined with tomatoes and melting mozzarella cheese, pasta makes a tasty filling for baked eggplant shells.

NUTRITIONAL INFORMATION

Calories 342	Sugars 6g
Protein 11g	Fat 16g
Carbohydrate . . . 40g	Saturates 4g

25 mins   55 mins

SERVES 4

INGREDIENTS

8 oz/225 g dried penne or other short pasta shapes

4 tbsp olive oil, plus extra for brushing

2 eggplants

1 large onion, chopped

2 garlic cloves, crushed

14 oz/400 g canned chopped tomatoes

2 tsp dried oregano

2 oz/55 g mozzarella cheese, thinly sliced

¼ cup freshly grated Parmesan cheese

2 tbsp dried bread crumbs

salt and pepper

salad greens, to serve

1 Bring a large pan of lightly salted water to a boil. Add the pasta and 1 tablespoon of the olive oil, bring back to a boil, and then cook for 8–10 minutes, or until tender but firm to the bite. Drain, return to the pan, cover, and keep warm.

2 Cut the eggplants in half lengthwise and score around the insides with a sharp knife, being careful not to pierce the shells. Scoop out the flesh with a spoon. Brush the insides of the shells with olive oil. Chop the flesh and set aside.

3 Heat the remaining oil in a skillet. Cook the onion until translucent. Add the garlic and cook for 1 minute, then add the chopped eggplant and cook, stirring frequently, for 5 minutes.

4 Add the chopped tomatoes and dried oregano to the pan, and season to taste with salt and pepper. Bring the mixture to a boil, then lower the heat and simmer for 10 minutes, or until it has thickened. Remove the pan from the heat and stir in the pasta.

5 Brush a cookie sheet with oil and arrange the eggplant shells in a single layer. Divide half of the tomato and pasta mixture between them. Scatter over the mozzarella slices, then pile the remaining tomato and pasta mixture on top. Mix the Parmesan and bread crumbs and sprinkle over, pressing lightly into the mixture.

6 Bake in a preheated oven, 400°F/ 200°C, for about 25 minutes, or until the topping is golden brown. Serve hot with a selection of mixed salad greens.

Pasta Omelet

This is a superb way of using up any leftover pasta, such as penne, macaroni, or conchiglie.

NUTRITIONAL INFORMATION

Calories 638	Sugars 5g	
Protein 24g	Fat 38g	
Carbohydrate ... 53g	Saturates 7g	

5 mins 15–20 mins

SERVES 2

INGREDIENTS

4 tbsp olive oil

1 small onion, chopped

1 fennel bulb, thinly sliced

generous 1 cup diced potato

1 garlic clove, chopped

4 eggs

1 tbsp chopped fresh flatleaf parsley

pinch of chili powder

3½ oz/100 g cooked short pasta

2 tbsp stuffed green olives, halved

salt and pepper

sprigs of fresh marjoram, to garnish

tomato salad, to serve

1 Heat half the oil in a heavy-bottomed skillet over low heat. Add the onion, fennel, and potato and cook, stirring occasionally, for 8–10 minutes, until the potato is just tender.

2 Stir in the chopped garlic and cook for 1 minute. Remove the pan from the heat, transfer the vegetables to a plate, and set aside to keep warm.

3 Beat the eggs until they are frothy. Stir in the parsley and season with salt, pepper, and a pinch of chili powder.

4 Heat 1 tablespoon of the remaining oil in a clean skillet. Add half of the egg mixture to the pan, then add the cooked vegetables, pasta, and half of the olives. Pour in the remaining egg mixture and cook until the sides begin to set.

5 Lift up the edges of the omelet with a spatula to allow the uncooked egg to spread underneath. Cook, shaking the pan occasionally, until the underside of the omelet is a light golden-brown color.

6 Slide the omelet out of the pan onto a plate. Wipe the pan with paper towels and heat the remaining oil. Invert the omelet into the pan and cook until the other side is golden brown.

7 Slide the omelet onto a warmed serving dish and garnish with the remaining olives and the marjoram. Serve cut into wedges, with a tomato salad.

Cheese, Nut & Pasta Salad

Use colorful salad greens to provide visual contrast to complement the variations in taste and texture.

NUTRITIONAL INFORMATION

Calories	694	Sugars	1g
Protein	22g	Fat	57g
Carbohydrate	24g	Saturates	15g

15 mins   15–20 mins

SERVES 4

INGREDIENTS

salt

8 oz/225 g dried pasta shells

1 tbsp olive oil

¾ cup shelled and halved walnuts

mixed salad greens, such as radicchio, escarole, arugula, corn salad, and frisée

8 oz/225 g dolcelatte cheese, crumbled

DRESSING

2 tbsp walnut oil

4 tbsp extra-virgin olive oil

2 tbsp red wine vinegar

salt and pepper

1 Bring a pan of lightly salted water to a boil. Add the pasta and olive oil and cook for 8–10 minutes, or until tender but firm to the bite. Drain, refresh under cold running water, drain again, and set aside.

2 Spread out the shelled walnut halves onto a cookie sheet and toast under a preheated broiler for 2–3 minutes. Set aside to cool while you make the dressing.

3 To make the dressing, whisk together the walnut oil, olive oil, and vinegar in a small bowl, and season to taste.

4 Arrange the salad greens in a large serving bowl. Pile the cooled pasta in the middle of the salad greens and sprinkle over the dolcelatte cheese. Just before serving, pour the dressing over the pasta salad, scatter over the walnut halves, and toss together to mix and to coat in the dressing. Serve immediately.

COOK'S TIP

Dolcelatte is a semisoft, blue-veined cheese from Italy. Its texture is creamy and smooth and the flavor is delicate, but piquant. You could use Roquefort instead. It is essential that whatever cheese you choose, it is of the best quality and in peak condition.

Garlic Mushroom Pizza

This pizza dough is flavored with garlic and herbs and topped with mixed mushrooms and melting cheese for a really delicious pizza.

NUTRITIONAL INFORMATION

Calories 541	Sugars 5g	
Protein 16g	Fat 15g	
Carbohydrate . . .91g	Saturates 6g	

🍲 45 mins   🕒 30 mins

SERVES 4

INGREDIENTS

DOUGH

3½ cups white bread flour, plus extra for dusting

2 tsp rapid-rise dry yeast

2 garlic cloves, crushed

2 tbsp chopped fresh thyme

2 tbsp olive oil, plus extra for greasing

1¼ cups lukewarm water

TOPPING

2 tbsp butter or margarine

4²/₃ cups sliced mixed mushrooms

2 garlic cloves, crushed

2 tbsp chopped fresh parsley, plus extra to garnish

2 tbsp tomato paste

6 tbsp sieved tomatoes

¾ cup grated mozzarella cheese

salt and pepper

1 Mix the flour, yeast, garlic, and thyme in a bowl. Make a well in the center and gradually stir in the oil and water. Bring together to form a soft dough.

2 Turn the dough onto a floured counter and knead for 5 minutes, or until smooth. Roll into a 14-inch/35-cm circle. Brush a cookie sheet with a little oil and place the dough base on it. Set aside in a warm place for 20 minutes, or until the dough puffs up.

3 Meanwhile, make the topping. Melt the butter or margarine in a skillet and cook the mushrooms, garlic, and parsley over low heat for 5 minutes.

4 Combine the tomato paste and sieved tomatoes and spoon onto the pizza base, leaving a ½-inch/1-cm border of dough. Spoon the mushroom mixture on top. Season to taste with salt and pepper and sprinkle over the cheese.

5 Cook the pizza in a preheated oven, 375°F/190°C, for 20–25 minutes, or until the bottom is crisp and the cheese has melted. Garnish with chopped parsley and serve the pizza immediately.

Patriotic Pasta

The ingredients of this dish have the same bright colors as the Italian flag—hence its name.

NUTRITIONAL INFORMATION	
Calories 325	Sugars 5g
Protein 8g	Fat 13g
Carbohydrate . . . 48g	Saturates 2g

 5 mins   🕑 15 mins

SERVES 4

I N G R E D I E N T S

1 lb/450 g dried farfalle

4 tbsp olive oil

1 lb/450 g cherry tomatoes

3 oz/90 g arugula

salt and pepper

romano cheese, to garnish

1 Bring a large pan of lightly salted water to a boil. Add the farfalle and 1 tablespoon of the olive oil and cook for 8–10 minutes, or until tender but still firm to the bite. Drain the farfalle thoroughly and return to the pan.

2 Cut the cherry tomatoes in half and trim the arugula.

3 Heat the remaining olive oil in a large pan. Add the tomatoes to the pan and cook for 1 minute. Add the farfalle and arugula to the pan and stir gently to mix. Heat the mixture through and season to taste with salt and pepper.

4 Meanwhile, using a vegetable peeler, shave thin slices of romano cheese.

5 Transfer the farfalle and vegetables to a warm serving dish. Garnish with the cheese shavings and serve immediately.

COOK'S TIP

Romano cheese is a hard sheep's milk cheese that resembles Parmesan, and is often used for grating over a variety of dishes. It has a sharp flavor and is only used in small quantities.

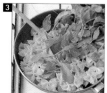

Vegetable Pasta Nests

These large pasta nests look impressive when presented filled with broiled mixed vegetables, and taste delicious.

NUTRITIONAL INFORMATION

Calories	392	Sugars	1g
Protein	6g	Fat	28g
Carbohydrate	32g	Saturates	9g

 25 mins 40 mins

SERVES 4

INGREDIENTS

6 oz/175 g spaghetti

1 eggplant, halved and sliced

1 zucchini, diced

1 red bell pepper, seeded and sliced diagonally

6 tbsp olive oil

2 garlic cloves, crushed

4 tbsp butter or margarine, melted

1 tbsp dried white bread crumbs

salt and pepper

sprigs of fresh parsley, to garnish

1 Bring a large pan of water to a boil. Add the spaghetti and cook for 8–10 minutes, or until tender but still firm to the bite. Drain the spaghetti and set aside until required.

2 Place the eggplant, zucchini, and bell pepper on a cookie sheet. Mix the oil and garlic together and pour over the vegetables, brushing to coat all over.

3 Cook the vegetables under a preheated hot broiler for about 10 minutes, turning, until tender and lightly charred. Set aside and keep warm.

4 Divide the spaghetti among 4 large, lightly greased muffin pans. Using 2 forks, arrange the spaghetti to form nests.

5 Brush the pasta nests with melted butter or margarine and sprinkle with bread crumbs. Bake in a preheated oven, 400°F/200°C, for 15 minutes, or until lightly golden. Remove the nests from the pans and transfer to serving plates. Divide the broiled vegetables between the nests, season, and garnish with parsley sprigs.

 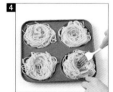 

Green Tagliatelle with Garlic

A rich pasta dish for garlic lovers everywhere. It is quick and easy to prepare, and full of flavor.

NUTRITIONAL INFORMATION

Calories 526   Sugars 3g
Protein .... 14g   Fat 34g
Carbohydrate ... 45g   Saturates 13g

5 mins   20 mins

SERVES 4

INGREDIENTS

2 tbsp walnut oil

1 bunch scallions, sliced

2 garlic cloves, thinly sliced

3⅓ cups sliced mushrooms

1 lb/450 g fresh green and white tagliatelle

1 tbsp olive oil

8 oz/225 g frozen spinach, thawed and drained

½ cup fullfat soft cheese with garlic and herbs

4 tbsp light cream

scant ½ cup chopped, unsalted pistachios

2 tbsp shredded fresh basil

sprigs of fresh basil, to garnish

fresh Italian bread, to serve

3 Meanwhile, bring a large pan of lightly salted water to the boil. Add the tagliatelle and olive oil and cook for 3–5 minutes, or until tender but still firm to the bite. Drain the tagliatelle thoroughly and return to the pan.

4 Add the spinach to the skillet and heat through for 1–2 minutes. Add the cheese to the pan and let it melt slightly. Stir in the cream and continue to cook, without letting the mixture boil, until warmed through.

5 Pour the sauce over the pasta, season to taste with salt and black pepper, and mix well. Heat through gently, stirring constantly, for 2–3 minutes.

6 Transfer the pasta to a serving dish and sprinkle over the pistachios and shredded basil. Garnish with the basil sprigs and serve immediately with the Italian bread of your choice.

1 Heat the walnut oil in a large skillet. Add the scallions and garlic and cook for 1 minute, until just softened.

2 Add the mushrooms to the pan, stir well, cover, and cook over low heat for about 5 minutes, until softened.

Spinach & Nut Pasta

Use any pasta shapes that you have for this recipe. Multicolored pasta is visually the most attractive.

NUTRITIONAL INFORMATION

Calories	603	Sugars	5g
Protein	12g	Fat	41g
Carbohydrate	46g	Saturates	6g

 5 mins   🕐 15 mins

SERVES 4

INGREDIENTS

8 oz/225 g dried pasta shapes

½ cup olive oil

2 garlic cloves, crushed

1 onion, cut into fourths and sliced

3 large flat mushrooms, sliced

8 oz/225 g spinach

2 tbsp pine nuts

6 tbsp dry white wine

salt and pepper

Parmesan shavings, to garnish

1 Cook the pasta in a pan of boiling salted water for 8–10 minutes, or until tender but still firm to the bite. Drain well.

2 Meanwhile, heat the oil in a large pan and cook the crushed garlic and sliced onion for 1 minute.

3 Add the sliced mushrooms to the pan and cook over medium heat, stirring occasionally, for 2 minutes.

4 Lower the heat, add the spinach to the pan, and cook, stirring occasionally, for 4–5 minutes, or until it has wilted.

5 Stir in the pine nuts and wine, season to taste, and cook for 1 minute.

6 Transfer the pasta to a warm serving bowl and toss the sauce into it, mixing well. Garnish with shavings of Parmesan cheese and serve.

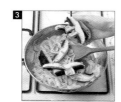

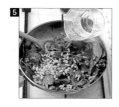

COOK'S TIP

Nutmeg has a particular affinity with spinach, so grate a little over this dish to give it extra flavor.

Spinach & Mushroom Lasagna

This is an extremely tasty vegetarian dish. For a variation you could substitute sliced roasted bell peppers for the spinach (see below).

NUTRITIONAL INFORMATION

Calories 720	Sugars 9g
Protein 31g	Fat 52g
Carbohydrate . . .36g	Saturates 32g

  20 mins   40 mins

SERVES 4

I N G R E D I E N T S

½ cup butter, plus extra for greasing

2 garlic cloves, finely chopped

4 oz/115 g shallots

8 oz/225 g wild mushrooms, such as chanterelles

1 lb/450 g spinach, cooked, drained, and finely chopped

2¼ cups grated colby cheese

¼ tsp freshly grated nutmeg

1 tsp chopped fresh basil

2 oz/55 g all-purpose flour

2½ cups hot milk

⅔ cup grated Cheshire cheese

8 sheets precooked lasagna

salt and pepper

1 Lightly grease a large ovenproof dish with a little butter.

2 Melt half of the butter in a pan. Add the garlic, shallots, and mushrooms, and cook over low heat for 3 minutes. Stir in the spinach, colby cheese, nutmeg, and basil. Season with salt and pepper to taste and set aside.

3 Melt the remaining butter in another pan over low heat. Add the flour and cook, stirring constantly, for 1 minute. Gradually stir in the hot milk, whisking

constantly, until smooth. Stir in ¼ cup of the Cheshire cheese and season to taste with salt and pepper.

4 Spread half of the mushroom and spinach mixture over the bottom of the prepared dish. Cover with a layer of lasagna, then with half of the cheese sauce. Repeat the process and sprinkle over the remaining Cheshire cheese.

5 Bake in a preheated oven, 400°F/200°C, for 30 minutes, or until golden brown. Serve the lasagna while it is still very hot.

VARIATION

You could substitute 4 bell peppers for the spinach. Roast in a preheated oven, 400°F/200°C, for 20 minutes. Rub off the skins under cold water, seed, and chop before using.

Pasta & Vegetable Sauce

The shapes and textures of the vegetables make a mouthwatering presentation in this light and summery dish.

NUTRITIONAL INFORMATION

Calories 389   Sugars 4g
Protein . . . . 16g   Fat 20g
Carbohydrate . . . 38g   Saturates 11g

10 mins   30 mins

SERVES 4

I N G R E D I E N T S

8 oz/225 g dried gemelli or other
  pasta shapes

1 tbsp olive oil

1 head green broccoli, cut into florets

2 zucchini, sliced

8 oz/225 g asparagus spears

4 oz/115 g snow peas

4 oz/115 g frozen peas

2 tbsp butter

3 tbsp vegetable bouillon

4 tbsp heavy cream

freshly grated nutmeg

2 tbsp chopped fresh parsley

2 tbsp freshly grated Parmesan cheese

salt and pepper

1 Bring a large pan of lightly salted water to a boil. Add the pasta and olive oil and cook for 8–10 minutes, or until tender but still firm to the bite. Drain, return to the pan, cover, and keep warm.

2 Steam the broccoli, zucchini, asparagus spears, and snow peas over a pan of boiling salted water until they are just beginning to soften, then remove from the heat and refresh in cold water. Drain and set aside.

3 Bring a small pan of lightly salted water to a boil. Add the frozen peas and cook for 3 minutes. Drain the peas, refresh in cold water, then drain again. Set aside with the other vegetables.

4 Melt the butter with the vegetable bouillon in a pan over medium heat. Add all the vegetables, reserving a few of the asparagus spears, and toss carefully with a wooden spoon until they have heated through, taking care not to break them up.

5 Stir in the cream and heat through without bringing to a boil. Season to taste with salt, pepper, and nutmeg.

6 Transfer the pasta to a warmed serving dish and stir in the chopped parsley. Spoon over the vegetable sauce and sprinkle over the Parmesan cheese. Arrange the reserved asparagus spears in a pattern on top and serve.

Fettuccine all'Alfredo

This simple, traditional dish can be made with any long pasta, but is especially good with flat noodles, such as fettuccine or tagliatelle.

NUTRITIONAL INFORMATION	
Calories 540	Sugars 2g
Protein 15g	Fat 40g
Carbohydrate ... 31g	Saturates 23g

🍥 🍥 🍥

🥔 5 mins   🕐 5 mins

SERVES 4

INGREDIENTS

2 tbsp butter

scant 1 cup heavy cream

1 lb/450 g fresh fettuccine

1 tbsp olive oil

scant 1 cup freshly grated Parmesan cheese, plus extra to serve

pinch of freshly grated nutmeg

salt and pepper

sprigs of fresh flatleaf parsley, to garnish

1 Put the butter and $^2/_3$ cup of the cream in a large pan and bring the mixture to a boil over medium heat. Lower the heat and simmer gently for about $1^1/_2$ minutes, or until slightly thickened.

2 Meanwhile, bring a large pan of lightly salted water to a boil. Add the fettuccine and olive oil and cook for 2–3 minutes, or until tender but still firm to the bite. Drain the fettuccine thoroughly and return it to the warm pan, then pour over the cream sauce.

3 Toss the fettuccine in the sauce over low heat until thoroughly coated.

4 Add the remaining cream and the Parmesan cheese and nutmeg to the fettuccine mixture, and season to taste with salt and pepper. Toss thoroughly to coat while gently heating through.

5 Transfer the fettuccine to a warm serving plate and garnish with fresh parsley. Serve immediately, handing extra grated Parmesan cheese separately.

VARIATION

This classic Roman dish is often served with the addition of strips of ham and fresh peas. Add $1^1/_2$ cups shelled cooked peas and 6 oz/175 g ham strips with the Parmesan cheese in step 4.

Italian Fish Stew

This robust stew is full of Mediterranean flavors. If you do not want to prepare the fish yourself, ask your local fish dealer to do it for you.

NUTRITIONAL INFORMATION

Calories 236	Sugars 4g	
Protein 20g	Fat 7g	
Carbohydrate ... 25g	Saturates 1g	

5–10 mins   25 mins

SERVES 4

INGREDIENTS

2 tbsp olive oil

2 red onions, finely chopped

1 garlic clove, crushed

2 zucchini, sliced

14 oz/400 g canned chopped tomatoes

3½ cups vegetable or fish bouillon

3 oz/90 g dried pasta shapes

12 oz/350 g firm white fish, such as cod, haddock, or hake

1 tbsp chopped fresh basil or oregano, or 1 tsp dried oregano

1 tsp grated lemon zest

1 tbsp cornstarch

1 tbsp water

salt and pepper

sprigs of fresh basil or oregano, to garnish

1 Heat the oil in a large pan and cook the onions and garlic for 5 minutes. Add the zucchini and continue to cook for 2–3 minutes, stirring often.

2 Add the tomatoes and bouillon to the pan and bring to a boil. Add the pasta, cover the pan, and lower the heat. Simmer for 5 minutes.

3 Skin and bone the fish, then cut it into chunks. Add the fish chunks to the pan with the herbs and lemon zest and cook gently for 5 minutes, until the fish is opaque and flakes easily (take care not to overcook it).

4 Blend the cornstarch with the water and stir into the stew. Cook gently for 2 minutes, stirring, until thickened. Season with salt and pepper to taste and ladle into warmed soup bowls. Garnish with sprigs of basil or oregano and serve at once.

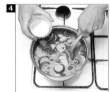

Smoked Haddock Casserole

This quick, easy, and inexpensive dish would be ideal for a midweek family supper.

NUTRITIONAL INFORMATION

Calories	525	Sugars	.........8g
Protein	........41g	Fat	..........18g
Carbohydrate	...53g	Saturates	......10g

20 mins   45 mins

SERVES 4

I N G R E D I E N T S

2 tbsp butter, plus extra for greasing

1 lb/450 g smoked haddock fillets, cut into 4 slices

2½ cups milk

2 tbsp all-purpose flour

pinch of freshly grated nutmeg

3 tbsp heavy cream

1 tbsp chopped fresh parsley

2 eggs, hard-cooked and mashed to a pulp

1 lb/450 g dried fusilli

1 tbsp lemon juice

salt and pepper

cooked new potatoes and beets, to serve

1 Thoroughly grease a casserole dish with butter. Put the haddock in the casserole and pour over the milk. Bake in a preheated oven, 400°F/200°C, for about 15 minutes. Carefully pour the cooking liquid into a pitcher without breaking up the fish.

2 Melt the 2 tablespoons of butter in a pan and stir in the flour. Gradually whisk in the reserved cooking liquid. Season to taste, with salt, pepper, and nutmeg. Stir in the cream, parsley, and mashed eggs and cook, stirring constantly, for 2 minutes.

3 Meanwhile, bring a large pan of lightly salted water to a boil. Add the fusilli and lemon juice and cook for 8-10 minutes, until tender but still firm to the bite.

4 Drain the pasta, and spoon or tip it over the fish. Top with the egg sauce and return the casserole to the oven for another 10 minutes.

5 Serve the fish casserole with boiled new potatoes and freshly cooked beets.

VARIATION

You can use any type of dried pasta for this casserole. Try penne, conchiglie, or rigatoni.

Fillets of Red Mullet & Pasta

In this recipe, a lemon and herb sauce perfectly complements the sweet flavor and delicate texture of the fish.

NUTRITIONAL INFORMATION

Calories 457	Sugars 3g	
Protein 39g	Fat 12g	
Carbohydrate ... 44g	Saturates 5g	

🐡 🐡 🐡

🍲 15 mins   🕐 1 hr

SERVES 4

INGREDIENTS

2 lb 4 oz/1 kg red mullet fillets

1¼ cups dry white wine

4 shallots, finely chopped

1 garlic clove, crushed

3 tbsp finely chopped fresh mixed herbs

finely grated zest and juice of 1 lemon

pinch of freshly grated nutmeg

3 anchovy fillets, roughly chopped

1 tbsp butter

2 tbsp heavy cream

1 tsp cornstarch

1 lb/450 g dried vermicelli

1 tbsp olive oil

salt and pepper

TO GARNISH

sprig of fresh mint

lemon slices

lemon zest

1 Put the red mullet fillets in a large casserole. Pour over the wine and add half the chopped shallots with the garlic, herbs, lemon zest and juice, nutmeg, and anchovies. Season, cover the casserole, and bake in a preheated oven, 350°F/180°C, for 35 minutes.

2 Carefully lift out the baked fish and transfer to a warm plate. Set the plate aside and keep warm. Strain and reserve the cooking liquid.

3 Heat the butter in a pan and cook the remaining shallots over low heat, stirring, for 5 minutes. Pour the cooking liquid into the pan and bring to a boil. Simmer for 25 minutes, until reduced by half. Mix the cream and cornstarch together and stir into the sauce to thicken.

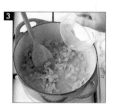

4 Meanwhile, bring a pan of lightly salted water to a boil. Add the vermicelli and oil and cook for 8–10 minutes, or until tender but still firm to the bite. Drain the pasta and transfer to a warm serving dish.

5 Arrange the fish fillets on top of the vermicelli and pour over the sauce. Garnish with a fresh mint sprig, slices of lemon, and strips of lemon zest, and serve immediately.

Seafood Lasagna

You can use any fish and any sauce you like in this recipe: try smoked haddock and whiskey sauce, or cod with cheese sauce.

NUTRITIONAL INFORMATION

Calories 790   Sugars 23g
Protein . . . . 55g   Fat 32g
Carbohydrate . . . 74g   Saturates 19g

30 mins   45 mins

SERVES 4

INGREDIENTS

1 lb/450 g smoked haddock, filleted, skin removed, and flesh flaked

4 oz/115 g shrimp, peeled and deveined

4 oz/115 g sole fillet, skin removed and flesh sliced

juice of 1 lemon

SAUCE

4 tbsp butter

3 leeks, very thinly sliced

scant ½ cup all-purpose flour

2½ cups milk

2 tbsp clear honey

2 cups grated mozzarella cheese

1 lb/450 g precooked lasagna

⅔ cup freshly grated Parmesan cheese

pepper

VARIATION

For a cider sauce, substitute 1 finely chopped shallot for the leeks, 1¼ cups hard cider and 1¼ cups heavy cream for the milk, and 1 teaspoon of mustard for the honey. For a Tuscan sauce, substitute 1 chopped fennel bulb for the leeks, and omit the honey.

1 Put the haddock fillet, shrimp, and sole fillet into a large bowl, season with pepper, and add lemon juice to taste. Cover the bowl and set it aside while you make the sauce.

2 Melt the butter in a large pan. Add the leeks and cook, stirring occasionally, for 8 minutes. Add the flour and cook, stirring constantly, for 1 minute. Gradually stir in enough milk to make a thick, creamy sauce.

3 Stir in the honey and mozzarella cheese and continue cooking for another 3 minutes. Remove the pan from the heat and mix in the fish and shrimp.

4 Arrange alternate layers of fish sauce and lasagna in an ovenproof dish, finishing with a fish sauce layer on top. Generously sprinkle over the grated Parmesan cheese and bake in a preheated oven, 350°F/180°C, for 30 minutes. Remove from the oven and serve immediately.

Linguine with Sardines

This is a very quick dish that is ideal for midweek suppers because it is so simple to prepare yet full of flavor.

NUTRITIONAL INFORMATION

Calories	547	Sugars	5g
Protein	23g	Fat	23g
Carbohydrate	68g	Saturates	3g

5–10 mins   10–15 mins

SERVES 4

INGREDIENTS

8 sardines, filleted

1 fennel bulb

4 tbsp olive oil

3 garlic cloves, sliced

1 tsp chili flakes

12 oz/350 g dried linguine

½ tsp finely grated lemon zest

1 tbsp lemon juice

2 tbsp pine nuts, toasted

2 tbsp chopped fresh parsley,
   plus extra to garnish

salt and pepper

1 Wash and dry the sardines. Roughly chop them into large pieces and set aside. Trim the fennel bulb, removing any tough outer leaves, and slice very thinly.

2 Heat 2 tablespoons of the olive oil in a large skillet and add the garlic and chili flakes. Cook for 1 minute then add the fennel. Cook over medium-high heat for 4–5 minutes, until softened. Add the sardine pieces and heat for another 3–4 minutes, until just cooked.

3 Meanwhile, cook the pasta in plenty of boiling salted water according to the package instructions, until tender but still firm to the bite. Drain well and return to the pan to keep warm.

4 Add the lemon zest and juice, pine nuts, parsley, and seasoning to the sardines and toss together. Add the mixture to the pasta with the remaining olive oil and toss together gently. Serve immediately with a sprinkling of parsley.

COOK'S TIP
Reserve a couple of tablespoons of the pasta cooking water and add it to the pasta with the sauce if the mixture seems a little dry.

Tagliatelle with Pumpkin

This unusual dish comes from the Emilia Romagna region. Why not serve it with Lambrusco, the local wine?

NUTRITIONAL INFORMATION

Calories 559	Sugars 7g	
Protein 17g	Fat 32g	
Carbohydrate . . . 55g	Saturates 14g	

5 mins   20–25 mins

SERVES 4

I N G R E D I E N T S

1 lb 2 oz/500 g pumpkin or butternut squash, peeled and seeded

3 tbsp olive oil

1 onion, finely chopped

2 garlic cloves, crushed

4–6 tbsp chopped fresh parsley

pinch of freshly grated nutmeg

1 cup vegetable or chicken bouillon

4 oz/115 g prosciutto, cut into small pieces

9 oz/250 g dried tagliatelle

⅔ cup heavy cream

salt and pepper

freshly grated Parmesan cheese, to serve

3 Add the pumpkin pieces and cook for 2–3 minutes. Season to taste with salt, pepper, and nutmeg.

4 Add half the bouillon to the pan, bring to a boil, cover, and simmer for about 10 minutes, or until the pumpkin is tender. Add more bouillon if the pumpkin is becoming dry and looks as if it might be about to burn.

5 Add the prosciutto to the pan and cook, stirring, for another 2 minutes.

6 Meanwhile, bring a large pan of lightly salted water to a boil. Add the tagliatelle and the remaining oil and cook for 12 minutes, or until tender but still firm to the bite. Drain the pasta and transfer to a warm serving dish.

7 Stir the cream into the pumpkin and prosciutto mixture and heat through well. Spoon the pumpkin mixture over the tagliatelle, sprinkle over the remaining parsley, and serve while still hot. Hand the grated Parmesan separately.

1 Cut the pumpkin or butternut squash in half and scoop out the seeds with a spoon. Cut the pumpkin or squash into ½-inch/1-cm cubes.

2 Heat 2 tablespoons of the olive oil in a large pan. Add the onion and garlic and cook over low heat for about 3 minutes, until soft. Add half the parsley and cook for 1 minute.

Chicken Suprême Spaghetti

The refreshing combination of chicken and orange sauce makes this a perfect dish for a warm summer evening.

NUTRITIONAL INFORMATION

Calories 933	Sugars 34g	
Protein 74g	Fat 24g	
Carbohydrate . . 100g	Saturates 5g	

5 mins   25 mins

SERVES 4

I N G R E D I E N T S

2 tbsp rapeseed oil

3 tbsp olive oil

4 chicken suprêmes, about 8 oz/225 g each

²/₃ cup orange brandy

2 tbsp all-purpose flour

²/₃ cup freshly squeezed orange juice

1 oz/25 g zucchini, cut into very thin strips

1 oz/25 g leek, finely shredded

1 oz/25 g red bell pepper, cut into very thin strips

14 oz/400 g dried whole-wheat spaghetti

3 large oranges, peeled and cut into segments

rind of 1 orange, cut into very thin strips

2 tbsp chopped fresh tarragon

scant ³/₄ cup ricotta cheese

salt and pepper

fresh tarragon leaves, to garnish

1 Heat the rapeseed oil and 1 tablespoon of the olive oil in a skillet. Add the chicken and cook quickly until golden brown. Add the orange brandy and cook for 3 minutes. Sprinkle over the flour and cook for 2 minutes.

2 Lower the heat and add the orange juice, zucchini, leek, and bell pepper, and season with salt and pepper. Simmer for 5 minutes, until the sauce has thickened.

3 Meanwhile, bring a pan of salted water to a boil. Add the spaghetti and 1 tablespoon of the olive oil and cook for 10 minutes. Drain, transfer to a serving dish, and drizzle over the remaining oil.

4 Add half the orange segments, half of the orange rind strips, the tarragon, and the ricotta cheese to the sauce in the pan, and cook for 3 minutes.

5 Place the chicken on top of the pasta, pour over a little sauce, garnish with the remaining orange segments and rind, and the tarragon, and serve immediately.

Slices of Duckling with Pasta

A raspberry and honey sauce superbly counterbalances the richness of tender slices of duckling in this dish.

NUTRITIONAL INFORMATION

Calories 686	Sugars 15g	
Protein 62g	Fat 20g	
Carbohydrate . . . 70g	Saturates 7g	

15 mins   25 mins

SERVES 4

I N G R E D I E N T S

4 boned breasts of duckling, about
   9½ oz/275 g each

2 tbsp butter

¼ cup finely chopped carrots

4 tbsp finely chopped shallots

1 tbsp lemon juice

⅔ cup meat bouillon

4 tbsp clear honey

¾ cup fresh or thawed frozen raspberries

3 tbsp all-purpose flour

1 tbsp Worcestershire sauce

14 oz/400 g fresh linguine

1 tbsp olive oil

salt and pepper

T O   G A R N I S H

sprigs of fresh flatleaf parsley

fresh raspberries

1 Trim and score the duck breasts with a sharp knife and season well all over. Melt the butter in a skillet, add the duck breasts, and cook them until they are lightly colored on both sides.

2 Add the carrots, shallots, lemon juice, and half the meat bouillon and simmer over low heat for 1 minute. Stir in half of the honey and half of the raspberries. Sprinkle over half of the flour and cook, stirring constantly, for 3 minutes. Season with pepper to taste and add the Worcestershire sauce.

3 Stir in the remaining bouillon and cook for 1 minute. Stir in the remaining honey and the rest of the raspberries and sprinkle over the remaining flour. Cook for another 3 minutes.

4 Remove the duck breasts and let the sauce simmer over very low heat.

5 Meanwhile, bring a large pan of lightly salted water to a boil. Add the linguine and oil and cook for 8–10 minutes, or until tender but firm to the bite. Drain and divide between individual plates.

6 Slice the duck breast lengthwise into ¼-inch/5-mm thick pieces. Pour a little sauce over the pasta and arrange the slices in a fan shape on top. Garnish with parsley and raspberries and serve at once.

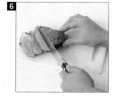